Wilkinson's Road Traffic Offences

WILKINSON'S ROAD TRAFFIC OFFENCES

SECOND SUPPLEMENT TO THE THIRTIETH EDITION

General Editor

KEVIN MCCORMAC O.B.E., M.A.
of Gray's Inn, Barrister,

PHILIP BROWN **M.A., LL.B.**
Former Senior Traffic Commissioner

MALCOLM DODDS **LL.M**
Deputy District Judge (Magistrates' Courts)

PETER VEITS
District Judge (Magistrates' Courts)

NICK WATSON **O.B.E., LL.M, M.B.A**
District Judge (Magistrates' Courts)

SWEET & MAXWELL

THOMSON REUTERS

Published in 2022 by Thomson Reuters, trading as Sweet & Maxwell.
(Registered in England & Wales, Company No 1679046.
Registered Office and address for service:
5 Canada Square, Canary Wharf, London E14 5AQ)

For further information on our products and services, visit
www.sweetandmaxwell.co.uk

Computerset by Sweet & Maxwell
Printed and bound in Great Britain by CPI Group (UK) Ltd,
Croydon, CR0 4YY

A CIP catalogue record for this book is available from the British Library.

ISBN (print) 978-0-414-11013-7

ISBN (e-book) 978-0-414-11015-1

ISBN (print and e-book) 978-0-414-11014-4

Crown copyright material is reproduced with the permission of the
Controller of HMSO and the King's Printer for Scotland.

TABLE OF CONTENTS

HOW TO USE THIS SUPPLEMENT

This is the Second Cumulative Supplement to the Thirtieth Edition of *Wilkinson's Road Traffic Offences* and has been compiled according to the structure of the main volume.

At the beginning of each chapter of this Supplement, a mini table of contents of the sections in the main volume has been included. Where a heading in this table of contents has been marked by a square pointer, this indicates that there is relevant information in this Supplement to which the reader should refer. Material that is new to the Cumulative Supplement is indicated by the symbol ■. Material that has been included from the previous supplement is indicated by the symbol □.

Within each chapter, updating information is referenced to the relevant paragraph in the main volume.

PREFACE

The law is generally stated as at 1 October 2022 although, as is our custom, we have worked to later dates in some instances.

Since the publication of the First Supplement to the 30th edition, we have seen the enactment and bringing into force of provisions affecting this work contained in the Police, Crime, Sentencing and Courts Act 2022 and the Judicial Review and Courts Act 2022. We have covered these provisions in the relevant places and they include important changes to the definition of a "competent and careful driver", increases in maximum penalties and minimum periods of disqualification for some offences where death is caused by bad driving, the introduction of a new offence of causing serious injury by careless driving and changes to the extension period for disqualification where a person is sentenced to seven years or more for a violent or sexual offence and so is not entitled to be released until two-thirds of the sentence has been completed. In the light of all these changes, it is pleasing to see that the Sentencing Council has consulted on revised guidelines and we anticipate being able to include the outcome in the 31st edition.

There is also a significant increase in the maximum penalty for obstructing a highway under the Highways Act 1980 making it an imprisonable offence, no doubt in response to recent changes in tactics of those protesting against various important current issues.

Changes to the Criminal Procedure Rules were made as usual in six-monthly stages and the most recent amendments helpfully included a more extensive description of circumstances in which an application for a summons or warrant will be refused.

Alongside further cases in relation to sentencing of those convicted of driving badly and causing death or serious injury, there have been some interesting cases on the appropriateness of disqualifying from driving those not actually driving a vehicle. In *R. v Wilson* [2022] EWCA Crim 807, a passenger who had shown reckless disregard for the rules of the road was disqualified and required to take an extended test and this was upheld on appeal as necessary for the protection of the public. In *R. v Khan* [2022] EWCA Crim 281 a defendant who had committed fraud in relation to the insuring of a vehicle and in falsely reporting it had been stolen was disqualified and this also was upheld on appeal. He had eventually admitted he was a passenger in a vehicle that had been driven dangerously but refused to name the driver. The courts seem more prepared than at times in the past to use this wide-ranging power.

I continue to be grateful to the editorial team who contribute with erudition and thoroughness as we seek to produce a work of the highest quality. Considerable thanks are also due to the staff at Sweet & Maxwell who provide professional support with regard to every aspect of production and publication.

Kevin McCormac
Worthing
November 2022

TABLE OF CASES

TABLE OF STATUTES

All entries are tabled to paragraph number

TABLE OF STATUTORY INSTRUMENTS

All entries are tabled to paragraph number

TABLE OF EU PROVISIONS

All entries are tabled to paragraph number

CHAPTER 1

DEFINITIONS

TABLE OF CONTENTS

MOTOR VEHICLES

"Intended or adapted for use on roads"

A   Go-carts, racing cars, powered transporters, etc.

As stated in the main work, an e-scooter is a sub-category of "motor vehicle" and **1-39** must comply with the criteria set out. Users must be licensed (category Q) and insured, must wear a cycle helmet and may not use the vehicle on a pavement. Use of e-scooters remains generally illegal, but the number of trial areas has been expanding. Although originally scheduled to end on 30 November 2021, the end date of the trial period was extended to 31 March 2022 as a result of the pandemic. As of February 2022, 31 regions were participating in the trials and the Government states that is undertaking "a comprehensive monitoring and evaluation programme". The latest Government guidance on the scheme is at *https://www.gov.uk/ guidance/e-scooter-trials-guidance-for-users* [Accessed 22 September 2022]. In the trial areas, e-scooters can be used on the same road space as cycles and electrically assisted pedal cycles (EAPCs: see para.1-23 in the main work). This means e-scooters are allowed on a road (except a motorway) and in cycle lanes and tracks, where possible. The controls over where e-scooters can be used are split between central government and local authorities and local authorities hosting trials need to ensure that their traffic regulation orders are updated and allow e-scooter use.

"ROAD"

Public access

1-141   Further consideration has been given to the way of assessing whether a means of access was a "road" in the civil case of *Bowen v Isle of Wight Council* [2021] EWHC 3254 (Ch) where the local council had decided that a privately owned way (known as Guildford Road) was not a road within the meaning of the Road Traffic Regulation Act 1984. This was important in the context of a planning application for development of an adjacent area. Guildford Road was a cul-de-sac on the north side of the public highway and there had never been any barrier or obstacle preventing access to it nor had there ever been a sign to show that the road was private and access was restricted. The evidence relevant to the case showed that the public had long exercised access. Local people used the road both with cars and on foot and parked their vehicles there when making use of the local amenities. It was common ground that Guildford Road was not a "highway" and that, as a matter of ordinary language, was a road. The key question was whether it was a "road to which the public has access". Although the general public accessed Guildford Road, the defendant, unsuccessfully, contended that the public access must be pursuant to an express or implied permission.

Following a detailed survey of the relevant case law, the judge concluded that public access fell within the terms of the definition of "road" (as set out in the main work) if that access was exercised with the permission of or the tolerance of the owner(s) of the road. Access by the public would still satisfy the definition provided it is not exercised in the face of, or in defiance of, efforts by the owner to prevent access. The judge concluded that a road will be a "road to which the public has access" (for the purposes of s.142 of the 1984 Act) provided that the general public, as an issue of fact, exercise access to it. This was subject to the qualification that those members of the public did not obtain access either by overcoming a physical obstruction or in defiance of prohibition. It was irrelevant to enquire further whether the presence of the public on the road was merely by the tolerance of the owners or whether the tolerance is to be taken to have given implicit permission.

CHAPTER 2

PROCEDURE

TABLE OF CONTENTS

COMMENCING PROCEEDINGS

The issue of a summons

As stated in the main work, the task for a magistrate (or approved legal adviser) **2-06** when considering an application by a private prosecutor for a summons (as restated in *R. (on the application of Kay) v Leeds Magistrates' Court* [2018] EWHC 1233 (Admin); [2018] 2 Cr. App. R. 27, summarising existing case law) is to ascertain whether the allegation is an offence known to the law, and, if so:

- whether the essential ingredients of the offence are prima facie present;
- that the offence alleged is not time-barred;
- that the court has jurisdiction; and
- whether the informant has the necessary authority to prosecute.

Where those tests are satisfied, generally the summons should be issued unless there are compelling reasons not to do so. The most obvious reasons are that the application is vexatious (which may involve the presence of an improper ulterior purpose and/or long delay), is an abuse of process or is otherwise improper. In considering those tests, the magistrate or legal adviser should consider the whole of the relevant circumstances in order to be satisfied that it is a proper case to issue the summons and, even if there is evidence of the offence, should consider whether the application is vexatious, an abuse of process, or otherwise improper. Whether the applicant has previously approached the police may be a relevant circumstance.

With effect from 3 October 2022, the Criminal Procedure Rules have been further amended by the like-named Amendment No.2 Rules 2022 (SI 2022/815). The most significant amendment is the insertion of a new r.7.2(14) setting out (non-exhaustive) examples of when a court may decline to issue a summons or warrant. This provision is set out below and, as will be seen, puts some detail into the previous criteria that provided for the application to be declined where it was vexatious, an abuse of process or otherwise improper. Rule 7.2(14) provides:

"(14) The court may decline to issue a summons or warrant if, for example—
(a) a court has previously determined an application by the same prosecutor

which alleged the same or substantially the same offence against the same defendant on the same or substantially the same asserted facts;

(b) the prosecutor fails to disclose all the information that is material to what the court must decide;

(c) the prosecutor has—

(i) reached a binding agreement with the defendant not to prosecute, or

(ii) made representations that no prosecution would be brought, on which the defendant has acted to the defendant's detriment;

(d) the prosecutor asserts facts incapable of proof in a criminal court as a matter of law;

(e) the prosecution would constitute an assertion that the decision of another court or authority was wrong where that decision has been, or could have been, or could be, questioned in other proceedings or by other lawful means; or

(f) the prosecutor's dominant motive would render the prosecution an abuse of the process of the court."

There is no obligation on the magistrate to make enquiries, but they may do so if they think it necessary and, as stated in the main work, a proposed defendant has no right to be heard, but there is a discretion to require the proposed defendant to be notified of the application and to hear the proposed defendant if thought necessary for the purpose of making a decision.

Rule 7.2(12) of the Criminal Procedure Rules 2020 (SI 2020/759), as amended, provides for a court to decide an application to issue or withdraw a summons without a hearing, which will generally be the case. Where the court decides to conduct a hearing, it may be in public or in private but the presumption is that it will be in private; it may only be in public if the court so directs. Where there is a hearing, the court does not have to invite the defendant to attend or to make representations. Where a party is to attend, it may do so in person, by live link or (following the most recent amendment to the Rules effective from 3 October 2022: SI 2022/815) by telephone.

In reviewing the prima facie evidence of the ingredients of the offence, the obligation is to conduct a rigorous analysis of the legal framework. In *R. (on the application of Johnson) v City of Westminster Magistrates' Court* [2019] EWHC 1709 (Admin); [2019] 1 W.L.R. 6238, the Divisional Court, in rejecting the submission that the threshold test for the issue of a summons was a low one, stressed the need for this review and rigorous analysis. In that case, the Magistrates' Court was held to have acted in excess of jurisdiction by unlawfully deciding to issue a summons where the ingredients of the offence (misconduct in public office contrary to common law) were not made out. In reiterating the requirement set out in *Kay*, the Divisional Court rejected the submission that this created a "low threshold". Indeed, in relation to the offence of misconduct in public office, the court observed that a failure to insist upon a high threshold, so as to confine that offence within its proper ambit, "would place a constraint upon the conduct of public officers in the proper performance of their duties, contrary to the public interest" (per Rafferty LJ at [24]).

In *R. (on the application of Smith-Allison) v Westminster Magistrates' Court (No.2)* [2021] EWHC 2361 (Admin), a duly authorised legal adviser had rejected an application for a summons, in part because it was considered to be more suited for civil proceedings (and there were related civil proceedings ongoing) and that there was no reasonable prospect of conviction. In upholding the applicant's appeal against that decision, the Divisional Court stated that the test for a person considering an application was not whether there was a realistic prospect of conviction but whether, given that the threshold requirements had been found to be met, the circumstances were such as to mean that there were compelling reasons for not issuing the summonses in this case. At this stage, it was no part of the test to evaluate the strength of the evidence further, provided that evidence of the essential elements of the offence in question had been found to be present and provided that the case was not so hopeless as to render the application vexatious or otherwise an abuse or improper.

As regards the potential civil proceedings, the legal adviser had formed the view that the fact that the parties were involved in civil proceedings rendered the prosecution improper and that was the only thing that had been identified as being improper in relation to the prosecution. The Divisional Court confirmed that existing case law makes clear that that was wrong. The fact of the civil proceedings may not have been an irrelevant consideration (in the sense that it was part of the background), but it was irrelevant to consider that recourse to relief in such proceedings meant that recourse to the criminal courts was improper.

Form of summons or requisition

The Criminal Procedure Rules 2020 (SI 2020/759) have been further amended, **2-12** most recently by the Criminal Procedure (Amendment No.2) Rules 2022 (SI 2022/815) effective from either 15 August 2022 or 3 October 2022. Rule 7(4) is amended to require a copy of a summons or requisition to be served on the parent or guardian of a person under the age of 18 as well as on the young person. Any requirement on the parent or guardian to attend may be included or may be subject to a separate summons or requisition. The Judicial Review and Courts Act 2022 has removed 21 statutory requirements for documents to be sent by post so that they can be served in accordance with Criminal Procedure Rules instead and this part of the Rules has been amended accordingly with effect from 15 August 2022.

Limitation of time

A further example of the application of the six-month time limit for summary- **2-42** only offences can be seen in *R. (on the application of Ogunsola) v Aylesbury Crown Court* [2021] EWHC 1062 (Admin); [2021] A.C.D. 81. The defendant had been charged with the indictable offences of voyeurism and trespassing with intent to commit a sexual offence; over a year had elapsed between the date of the offence and charge. When he appeared before the Crown Court, the judge acceded to a prosecution application to constitute himself as a district judge (magistrates' court) whereupon a new (summary-only) offence of harassment was put to the defendant who pleaded guilty to it. Upholding the defendant's appeal, the Divisional Court reaffirmed the requirement that a new summary-only offence must be commenced within the requisite time limit, here six months. As noted at para.2-85 in the main work, where an information had been laid within the six-month period, it could be amended after the expiry of that period, even to allege a different offence, provided the different offence alleged the same misdoing as the originally charged offence, and the amendment was in the interests of justice.

THE HEARING

The court

2-59   The Criminal Procedure Rules 2020 (SI 2020/759) have been further amended. The Criminal Procedure (Amendment No.2) Rules 2021 (SI 2021/849) effective from 4 October 2021 made changes which have the effect that the reference to r.5.8 in the main work should now be read as a reference to rr.5.7-5.11.

Refusal to hear a case

2-69   There has been further clarification of the extent to which a magistrates' court has no power to refuse to hear a case on the ground of abuse of process: *Mansfield v DPP* [2021] EWHC 2938 (Admin); [2022] Crim. L.R. 163. The Divisional Court stated that the class of abuse case falling to be decided exclusively in the High Court is very narrow and perhaps comprised only executive misconduct in relation to extradition. What appeared clear was that a magistrates' court would be competent to investigate and determine a wide range of circumstances arising from and bearing upon the fairness of the criminal process. It was clear that that jurisdiction would encompass instances where the police gave an assurance and then withdrew it, as in the instant case.

Proof of service; attendance of defendant

2-79   In relation to the making of statutory declarations, the provisions in the Criminal Procedure Rules 2020 (SI 2020/759) have been brought together under a new r.2.11 by the like-named Amendment No.2 Rules 2022 (SI 2022/815) effective from 3 October 2022. These provisions were previously in rr.29.4 and 44.2 of the Criminal Procedure Rules 2020.

Autrefois acquit or convict and pleas in bar

2-118   Further consideration was given to the circumstances where a defendant could successfully plead an abuse of process in *R. v Dunn* [2021] EWCA Crim 439. A defendant had been charged with conspiracy to facilitate the breach of immigration law and with taking part in the criminal activities of an organised crime group. At trial, the jury had failed to agree on the first charge but convicted on the second. On a second trial on the first charge, the defendant sought to persuade the court to stop the trial as an abuse of process because the subject matter was overlapping. Whilst the judge accepted that there was considerable overlap and the factual scenario was the same, nonetheless the offences were legally distinct and the argument was rejected. Upholding the decision of the judge, the Court of Appeal agreed that the offences were not "properly mutually exclusive alternatives" but had different elements that were beyond what could be considered as de minimis.

Summary trial: speeches and no case to answer

2-138   Rule 24.4 of the Criminal Procedure Rules 2020 (SI 2020/759) has been further amended. The effect of changes made by the Criminal Procedure (Amendment No.2) Rules 2021 (SI 2021/849) is that r.24.4(3) now provides not only for a witness to take an oath or be affirmed (unless legislation allows for a different procedure) but also, before the witness gives evidence, for the party who introduces the witness' evidence to explain how that evidence is admissible, unless it is only evidence of fact within the witness' direct knowledge.

The Judicial Review and Courts Act 2022 gives the Crown Court new powers to send a case back to the magistrates' court for trial or sentence. With effect from 28 April 2022, s.11 of the 2022 Act has amended both the Senior Courts Act 1981 (by inserting a new s.46ZA) and the Sentencing Code to enable a Crown Court to remit a youth or adult offender to a magistrates' court. For an adult offender, this may be after committal for sentence or conviction on indictment whereas, for a youth offender, it will only be available after committal for sentence. The Crown Court must take account of any other offence before the Crown Court (for any defendant) and the relevant allocation guidelines. Amendments have also been made to the Criminal Procedure Rules 2020 (SI 2020/759) by the like-named Amendment No.2 Rules 2022 (SI 2022/815) to facilitate the exercise of this power.

CHAPTER 3

EVIDENCE

Bad character

3-29   The Court of Appeal considered the issue of the admission of the underlying facts of a previous conviction for dangerous driving in *R. v Dabycharum* [2021] EWCA Crim 1923.

The defendant was facing a charge of wounding with intent under s.18 of the Offences Against the Persons Act 1861. He had earlier pleaded guilty to driving whilst disqualified and no insurance. He had deliberately driven his car into the complainant. The issue in trial became whether his previous conviction, for which he received the disqualification, namely dangerous driving, should be admitted and whether the facts of that offence should also be admitted. It was common ground that the fact that the defendant was disqualified from driving should be known to the jury. He had needed this to explain why he lied to the police that he was not the driver who had driven at the complainant causing injury. The defendant and complainant were known to each other but had fallen out some time before the incident.

The court ruled that the conviction and its underlying facts had become important explanatory evidence for the purposes of ss.101(1)(c) and 102(a) and (b) of the Criminal Justice Act 2003. The jury had been given evidence of the disqualification and were always likely to speculate about the reasons for the disqualification. It was important for the jury, in understanding the case as a whole, to know exactly what had occurred so that they could assess the explanations given. It would therefore not be reasonable to exclude that evidence under s.78 of the Police and Criminal Evidence Act 1984. The judge had properly directed the jury that the defendant's misconduct in the past could not in itself prove that he is guilty.

The case also considered the effect of the lies told by the defendant that he was not the driver. The judge had given a full direction under s.34 and gave clear directions both as to lies and the failure to mention matters in interview. The judge had properly drawn the attention of the jury to the issue by stating "In considering the above, you will want to bear in mind his explanation for not putting this forward, namely that he was scared to admit being the driver because he was disqualified, and that by the time of the interview he was being questioned for attempted murder".

CHAPTER 4

DRINK/DRIVING OFFENCES

Table of Contents

Sentencing, Procedure and Trial

Sentencing guidelines

The Sentencing Council has issued a consultation paper on guidelines for motoring offences and two offences covered in this chapter are included, those being: **4-320**

- Driving or attempting to drive with a specified drug above the specified limit, and
- Being in charge of a motor vehicle with a specified drug above the specified limit.

The consultation closed on the 29 September 2022 and any new guidelines published will feature in the 31st Edition.

Draft guidelines cannot be used in sentencing.

CHAPTER 5

DANGEROUS, CARELESS AND INCONSIDERATE DRIVING, ETC.

TABLE OF CONTENTS

DANGEROUS DRIVING

What is dangerous driving?

5-04   In the main work, reference is made to the difficulties that a court faces when assessing the standard of driving of a person who is a member of the emergency services responding to an emergency call. In response to this, the Police, Crime, Sentencing and Courts Bill contains an amendment to the test of what constitutes dangerous driving in such circumstances. If enacted in the form available at the time of writing, there will be a separate test for a "designated person" who is driving for police purposes (or, in the case of an NCA officer, law enforcement purposes) and has completed any prescribed training. This test is extended to include those who are training those who will be driving for police or law enforcement purposes. In such a situation, the test is based on what would be expected of a "competent and careful constable who has undertaken the prescribed training" rather than the "competent and careful driver".

Alternative verdicts

5-21   In the main work there is a table of alternative verdicts that are available under s.24(1) of the Road Traffic Offenders Act 1988.

This table is amended by Sch.8 to the Police, Crime, Sentencing and Courts Act 2022 by inserting the following:

Police, Crime, Sentencing and Courts Act 2022 Sch.8 para.2(2)

Road Traffic Offenders Act 1988 (c. 55)

2.—(2) In section 24 (alternative verdicts: general), in subsection (1), in the table—

(a) in the entry relating to section 1A of the Road Traffic Act 1988 (causing serious injury by dangerous driving), in the second column, after "Section 2 (dangerous driving)" insert "Section 2C (causing serious injury by careless, or inconsiderate, driving)", and

(b) after the entry relating to section 2B of that Act (causing death by careless, or inconsiderate, driving), insert—

"Section 2C (causing serious injury by careless, or inconsiderate, driving)	Section 3 (careless, and inconsiderate, driving"

The effect of this is that, when considering an offence of causing serious injury by dangerous driving, the court may, as an alternative, find the offender guilty of causing serious injury by careless driving and, for the new offence of causing serious injury by careless driving, an alternative verdict is careless driving.

There is also an omission from this table in the main work in that, after the entry for s.2 (dangerous driving), the next entry should be:

Section 2B (causing death by careless or inconsiderate driving)	Section 3 (careless, and inconsiderate, driving)

For completeness the full amended table as it applies to this chapter is produced below.

Section 1 (causing death by dangerous driving)	Section 2 (dangerous driving)
	Section 2B (causing death by careless or inconsiderate driving)
	Section 3 (careless, and inconsiderate, driving)
Section 1A (causing serious injury by dangerous driving)	Section 2 (dangerous driving)
	Section 2C (causing serious injury by careless or inconsiderate driving)
	Section 3 (careless, and inconsiderate, driving)
Section 2 (dangerous driving)	Section 3 (careless, and inconsiderate, driving)
Section 2B (causing death by careless or inconsiderate driving)	Section 3 (careless, and inconsiderate, driving)
Section 2C (causing serious injury by careless or inconsiderate driving)	Section 3 (careless, and inconsiderate, driving)
Section 3ZC (causing death by driving; disqualified drivers)	Section 103(1)(b) (driving whilst disqualified)
Section 3ZD (causing serious injury by driving; disqualified drivers)	Section 103(1)(b) (driving whilst disqualified)

Section 3A (causing death by careless driving when under the influence of drink or drugs)	Section 2B (causing death by careless or inconsiderate driving)
	Section 3 (careless, and inconsiderate, driving)
	Section 4(1) (driving when unfit to drive through drink or drugs)
	Section 5(1)(a) (driving with excess alcohol in breath, blood or urine)
	Section 7(6) (failing to provide specimen)
	Section 7A(6) (failing to give permission for laboratory test)

CAUSING DEATH BY DANGEROUS DRIVING

Evidence and procedure

5-36   The issue of causation in cases of causing death by dangerous driving has been covered in many cases covered in the main work at paras 5-28 to 5-36. The issue has again been considered in the case of *R. v Muhammed* [2021] EWCA Crim 802; [2021] 2 Cr. App. R. 17.

This was an appeal against convictions for causing death by dangerous driving, causing serious injury by dangerous driving and causing death by driving whilst uninsured. The defendant was driving his vehicle at a speed of approximately 100 miles per hour and was closely followed by another vehicle travelling at similar speed. Witnesses described the two vehicles as racing and thought that an accident was inevitable. Both were driving close to each other in the outside lane and did not attempt to move over. The defendant's car suffered a blowout of a rear tyre and his vehicle careered across the motorway and down an embankment where it collided with a tree. His wife and 11-year-old daughter were seriously injured and his three-year-old son died. There was an issue over whether the son had been properly restrained in his car seat.

The issues at trial were of causation; did his driving at speed cause the accident following the tyre blowout and did the lack of restraint of the son contribute to the vehicle being dangerous? The judge rejected submissions of no case to answer and subsequently the jury convicted on all counts.

The prosecution case had been based on the excessive speed, the poor condition of the 16-year-old tyre that had the blowout and the lack of proper restraint of the son. Tyre experts gave evidence and agreed that the vehicle had been travelling at speeds over 100 mph and that the tyre had visible signs of deterioration. It was accepted that the blowout could have occurred at 70 mph. The defendant had been evasive in interview about whether he checked the condition and pressure of the tyres, saying that they were checked professionally every two weeks, but did not say who carried out those checks.

The Court of Appeal were in no doubt that the judge had been correct in rejecting the submission of no case to answer as there was evidence from which the jury could conclude that the defendant was driving competitively, that being the driving at a speed greatly more than the speed limit and refusing to concede the outer lane to the car travelling some 10 metres behind him. The jury would be entitled to conclude that the manner of driving fell far below the standard of a careful and competent driver. Any defence of duress arising from the manner of driving of the other driver would be a matter for the jury. The judge had also correctly identified that the question of the seat belt deficiencies could establish dangerous driving in the appropriate context.

The appeal court reviewed the authorities referred to at para.5-35 of the main work, notably *R. v Girdler* [2009] EWCA Crim 2666; [2010] R.T.R. 28, and *R. v A* [2020] EWCA Crim 407; [2020] 2 Cr. App. R. 3. The conclusion was that the convictions were safe in that the defendant's credibility as to the state of knowledge of the roadworthiness of his car, the efficacy and utilisation of the rear seat belt restraints, the manner of driving and the issue of duress were live issues in the case. They were matters for the jury, as was their assessment of the factual causation of the tragic consequences that followed. The judge had summed up correctly and appropriately directed the jury.

DANGEROUS, CARELESS AND INCONSIDERATE DRIVING

Definition of careless or inconsiderate driving

In the main work, reference is made to the difficulties that a court faces when assessing the standard of driving of a person who is a member of the emergency services responding to an emergency call. In response to this, the Police, Crime, Sentencing and Courts Act 2022 contains an amendment to the test of what constitutes careless driving in such circumstances. Sections 5, 6 and 7 of the 2022 Act make amendments to the 1988 Act.   **5-51**

Section 2A of the 1988 Act (meaning of dangerous driving) is amended to provide a different test for those driving for police purposes who have undertaken prescribed training.

The new s.1B states that a designated person is to be regarded as driving dangerously if (and only if):

(a)   the way the person drives falls far below that would be expected of a competent and careful constable who has undertaken the prescribed training, and

(b)   it would be obvious to such a competent and careful constable that driving in that way would be dangerous.

Designated persons are defined to include constables and police staff including the national crime agency.

Similar amendments are made by s.6 of the 2022 Act by amending the definition of careless driving in s.3ZA of the 1988 Act.

Again the test applies to a designated person who is driving for police purposes and has undertaken the prescribed training.

The designated person is then to be regarded as driving without due care and attention if (and only if) the way the person drives falls below what would be expected of a competent and careful constable who has undertaken the prescribed training.

At the time of writing no implementation date has been set for these provisions.

Highway Code

Important changes to the Highway Code were announced on the 29th January 2022. The updated code is available at *https://www.gov.uk* or can be purchased from bookstores from April 2022. These are the key changes.   **5-81**

[13]

1. *Rule H1 deals with the Hierarchy of Road users* This places those most at risk in the event of a collision at the top of the hierarchy. It does not remove the need for everyone to behave responsibly and stresses the need for all road users to:
    *   be aware of the Highway Code;
    *   be considerate to other road users;
    *   understand their responsibility for the safety of others.

2. *Rule H2 deals with people crossing the road at junctions with more detail in rules 170, 195 and 206* When people are crossing or waiting to cross at a junction, other traffic should give way. If people have started crossing and traffic wants to turn into the road, the people crossing have priority and the traffic should give way.

    People driving, riding a motorcycle or cycling must give way to people on a zebra crossing and people walking and cycling on a parallel crossing.

3. *Rules 13, 62 and 63 deals with cyclists using the road with rules 67 and 213 giving further guidance* This gives guidance to cyclists riding in shared areas such as designated walkways and pavements with shared areas.

4. *Rules 67 and 213 give guidance to cyclists on positioning in the road* Cyclists may ride in the centre of their lane on quiet roads, in slower moving traffic and at the approach to junctions or road narrowing.

    Cyclists should keep at least 0.5 metres away from the kerb and further when safer, when riding on busy roads with vehicles moving faster than them.

    There is also guidance for those cycling in groups, in that they can cycle two abreast, but should also be conscious of other traffic and allow them to overtake.

5. *Rules 67, 76 163 212 and 215 deal with overtaking when driving or cycling* This provides updated guidance on safe passing distances and speeds for people driving or riding a motorcycle when overtaking vulnerable road users:
    *   leave at least 1.5 metres when overtaking people cycling at speeds of up to 30 mph, and give them more space when overtaking at higher speeds;
    *   pass people riding horses or driving horse drawn vehicles at speeds under 10 mph and allow at least 2 metres of space;
    *   allow at least 2 metres of space and keeping to a low speed when passing people walking in the road;
    *   wait behind them and not overtake if it is unsafe or not possible to meet these clearances.

6. *Further guidance for cyclists is dealt with in rules, 73, 74, 75, 76, 167, 170 and 211* This clarifies that, when turning at junctions, people cycling should give way to pedestrians who are walking or waiting to cross in a similar way to motorists. The code also clarifies that where there are no separate facilities for cyclists at junctions, they should position themselves in the centre of a lane in order to make themselves as visible as possible and avoid being overtaken where this would be dangerous.

7. *Rules 79, 167 and 186 give guidance on using roundabouts for cyclists, horse riders or horse drawn vehicles* This change clarifies that people driving or riding a motorcycle should give priority to those cycling at roundabouts. They should:

- not attempt to overtake people cycling within that person's lane;
- allow people cycling to move across their path as they travel around the roundabout

8. *Rules 239 deals with parking, leaving vehicles and people charging electric cars.* Guidance suggests using the "Dutch reach" when opening doors as this, by using the left hand to open the driver's door, makes people turn.

It also advises those charging electric cars to park as close to the charging point as possible to avoid trip hazards, display a warning sign if possible, and return charging cables neatly.

PENALTIES AND SENTENCING

Table of penalties

Changes to maximum sentences for certain offences have been brought into force   **5-130**
in relation to offences committed on or after 28 June 2022 by the Police, Crime, Sentencing and Courts Act 2022. The effect of these changes on the offences described in this chapter is to:

a) increase the maximum penalty for causing death by dangerous driving from 14 years to life imprisonment, by virtue of s.86(2) of the 2022 Act;

b) increase the maximum penalty for causing death by careless driving whilst under the influence of drink or drugs from 14 years to life imprisonment by virtue of s.86(3) of the 2022 Act.

In addition, and also from 28 June 2022, the Act created a new offence of causing serious injury by careless driving by inserting a new s.2C into the Road Traffic Act 1988:

Causing serious injury by careless, or inconsiderate, driving
2C.—(1)   A person who causes serious injury to another person by driving a mechanically propelled vehicle on a road or other public place without due care and attention, or without reasonable consideration for other persons using the road or place, is guilty of an offence.
(2)   In this section "serious injury" means—
(a) in England and Wales, physical harm which amounts to grievous bodily harm for the purposes of the Offences against the Person Act 1861, and
(b) in Scotland, severe physical injury.

The offence is triable either way with a maximum punishment on indictment of two years' imprisonment or a fine or both and carries both obligatory endorsement and disqualification by virtue of s.87(1) of the 2022 Act.

SENTENCING GUIDELINES

Generally

The Sentencing Council has published a consultation on proposed sentencing   **5-139**
guidelines for all the main road traffic offences covered in this chapter. The consultation is available at *https://www.sentencingcouncil.org.uk* [Accessed 23 September 2022].
The offences covered are:

- Causing death by dangerous driving

- Causing death by careless driving
- Causing death by careless driving under the influence of drink or drugs
- Causing death by driving whilst disqualified
- Causing death by driving whilst unlicensed or uninsured
- Dangerous driving
- Causing serious injury by dangerous driving
- Causing serious injury by careless driving
- Causing serious injury by driving whilst disqualified
- Causing injury by wanton or furious driving
- Driving or attempting to drive with a specified drug above the prescribed limit
- Being in charge of a motor vehicle with a specified drug above the prescribed limit

The consultation closed on 29 September 2022. Any new guidelines published will appear in the 31st Edition.

As with all draft guidelines, they are not to be used when sentencing.

Causing death by dangerous driving, causing death by careless driving when under the influence of drink or drugs, causing death by careless driving, and causing death by driving: unlicensed, disqualified or uninsured drivers

Death by careless driving: Sentencing cases

5-153   It is worth noting also that the CPS have updated their charging guidance on driving offence (see *https://www.cps.gov.uk/crime-info/driving-offences*).

Examples of dangerous driving are:

- racing, going too fast, or driving aggressively
- ignoring traffic lights, road signs or warnings from passengers
- overtaking dangerously
- driving under the influence of drink or drugs, including prescription drugs
- driving when unfit, including having an injury, being unable to see clearly, not taking prescribed drugs, or being sleepy
- knowing the vehicle has a dangerous fault or unsafe load
- the driver being avoidably and dangerously distracted, for example by:
  — using a handheld phone or other equipment
  — reading or looking at a map
  — talking to and looking at a passenger
  — lighting a cigarette, changing a CD or tape, tuning the radio

Examples of careless or inconsiderate driving are:

- overtaking on the inside
- driving too close to another vehicle
- driving through a red light by mistake
- turning into the path of another vehicle
- the driver being avoidably distracted by tuning the radio, lighting a cigarette, etc
- flashing lights to force other drivers to give way
- misusing lanes to gain advantage over other drivers
- unnecessarily staying in an overtaking lane
- unnecessarily slow driving or braking

- dazzling other drivers with undipped headlight

Death by careless driving whilst under the influence of drink or drugs, whilst unlicensed, uninsured or disqualified: sentencing cases

Sentencing in a case of causing death by careless driving whilst over the specified limit contrary to s.3A(1)(ba) of the Road Traffic Act 1988 was the issue in in *R. v Redding* [2021] EWCA Crim 1502. **5-176**

The defendant had been driving his van on a single carriageway road when he was blinded by sunlight and sadly collided with the deceased who was wheeling her bicycle along the roadside. There were no other aggravating factors, he was driving at 30 mph and stopped at the scene and called for assistance. There were no faults in the van, but he was found to have a level of 7 in Delta-9-tetrahydrocannabinol (THC) against the prescribed limit of 2. It was agreed, however, that the level of drugs was not a contributing factor to the collision.

The defendant was sentenced to two years' imprisonment suspended for two years with 170 hours of unpaid work and 15 rehabilitation activity days. He was also disqualified for two years and required to complete an extended driving test.

The Attorney General appealed the sentence as unduly lenient.

It was conceded that the judge may not have used the correct guidelines for the offence as he had not had his attention drawn to *R. v Mohammed* [2018] EWCA Crim 596; [2020] 4 W.L.R. 1, *R. v Myers* [2018] EWCA Crim 1974; [2019] 1 Cr. App. R. (S.) 6 and *R. v Adebisi* [2020] EWCA Crim 1446; [2021] 1 Cr. App. R. (S.) 61 (the first two covered in para 5-174 of the main work) which state that the guideline for s.3A of the 1988 Act applies to the offence under s.3A(1)(ba) even though the amendment to the legislation was made after the guideline.

The sentence was found not to be unduly lenient as the judge had still started from a starting point of three years which was within the range of the guideline as, for a moderate quantity of drugs, in the correct guideline the range was three to seven years.

There could not be proved a causal link between the level of cannabis and the nature of his driving. This was not a prolonged course of bad driving; it was a matter of seconds and the deceased would have been in a dark area by reason of the blinding sunlight. The absence of impairment was but one factor that permitted a sentence at the lower end of the range.

Death by dangerous driving: Sentencing cases

In *R. v Bennett* [2021] EWCA Crim 1838, the Court of Appeal dismissed an application by the Attorney General to review as unduly lenient a sentence of five years' imprisonment for two counts of causing death by dangerous driving. **5-197**

The defendant had been driving his lorry on the M56 motorway and collided with the rear of a Toyota whereupon the driver and front seat passenger, a married couple nearing retirement, were killed. The defendant had, it seems, been distracted by his mobile phone that he was using as a navigation aid and unplugged then replugged it and therefore did not see the queueing traffic until the last minute. There was discussion at the sentencing court as to whether the offence fell within level two or three of the guidelines. The Court of Appeal concluded that the sentencing judge had been correct in deciding that the case fell on the cusp between levels two and three. The judge had been entitled to conclude that whilst the offending was serious, the avoidable distraction could not be said to be gross. He had not been texting or reading and the distraction was for a brief period. The starting point of four years, therefore, was correct, but the aggravating factors of two deaths and injuries to others caused by the dangerous driving, together with a previous conviction for a mobile phone offence, increased the starting point to six years. After credit for guilty plea therefore, the sentence of five years could not be said to be unduly lenient.

In *R. v Hughes* [2022] EWCA Crim 538, the defendant was sentenced to 12 years' imprisonment for an offence of causing death by dangerous driving. He also received two concurrent sentences of three years for causing serious injury by dangerous driving.

The defendant drove his Ford Focus into the side of a taxi being driven by the deceased which was pulling out of a car park. Witnesses had described the Focus as screaming past them and CCTV showed that he was travelling at 56 mph when 220m from the collision site. The taxi driver died from his injuries and his two passengers suffered serious injuries. The defendant ran away from the scene but he was traced by DNA on the air bag and a bank card in the footwell.

In sentencing, the judge concluded that the case fell at the top end of level 1 of the guidelines and that, had he been convicted by a jury, he would have received the maximum sentence of 14 years' imprisonment. With a 15% guilty plea discount, he was given a sentence of 12-and-a-half years (he had pleaded guilty three months before his trial but had protested his innocence for a prolonged period claiming to have been a rear seat passenger).

On appeal, the sentence was reduced to a starting point of 12-and-a-half years, with 15% credit for guilty plea leading to a sentence of 10 years and 7 months. Given the statutory maximum of 14 years, the Court of Appeal had viewed the starting point as excessive since, sadly, the Court considered that there will be more serious cases than this.

The disqualification of 10 years was unchanged; however, the extension period was reduced to reflect the shorter custodial sentence.

In *R. v Todor* [2022] EWCA Crim 512, the defendant appealed against his sentence of eight years' imprisonment for an offence of causing death by dangerous driving.

He had been driving his HGV on a familiar route when he overtook a cyclist near a bend and in doing so crossed the central solid white lines. The deceased had been riding his motorcycle in the opposite direction following two cars. Those cars managed to take evasive action and braked and moved to the left side, but the deceased braked but collided with the rear of the second car and fell into the road and the rear tyre of the HGV brushed his helmet causing catastrophic brain injuries. He died a few days later in hospital.

The defendant had left the scene and was convicted after trial. He had maintained that he was blinded by the sun and had not seen the cyclist till the last minute and also sought to blame the deceased for not being able to brake in time.

Dash cam evidence was clear that the defendant could see the cyclist for some seven seconds, and that he had completed a similar manoeuvre some two hours earlier on the same stretch of road.

In dismissing the appeal against sentence, the Court stated that:

"It is important not to lose sight of the overall description, which is driving that involved a deliberate decision to ignore or a flagrant disregard for the rules of the road and an apparent disregard for greater danger being caused to others. The judge considered, in our view correctly, that although the period was relatively short (some 15 seconds) it undoubtedly involved a decision to ignore the rules of the road. This was not a few seconds across a white line by a driver in an ordinary saloon car; this was a huge vehicle being driven by an experienced driver across the white lines in such a position that it was certain that a car coming in the other direction would be in great peril."

The Court therefore concluded that the judge was justified in placing the offence within level 1 and the sentence was therefore to stand.

In *R. v Chorlton* [2022] EWCA Crim 934 the defendant appealed against a sentence of 10 years' imprisonment for an offence of causing death by dangerous driving.

He had been driving a Ford Focus with three passengers on board. He was seen driving at speed and performing handbrake turns. He drove out of a cul de sac and collided with an Audi and this caused the Focus to spin around and collide with some metal fencing. The deceased was thrown from the rear seat of the Focus and was found partially underneath the car and the defendant and other passengers fled the scene. He subsequently handed himself in to the police and later pleaded guilty to the offence some six months after his initial not guilty plea.

The judge placed the offence in level 1 as he had demonstrated a total disregard for the rules of the road. He was already on suspended sentence for an offence of dangerous driving and was on bail for another offence of driving whilst disqualified and being uninsured.

The starting point was therefore 12 years and that was reduced by 15% to reflect the guilty plea hence reducing the sentence to 10 years.

The appeal court confirmed that the starting point in level 1 was correct. The actual driving may have been in level 2 but the previous convictions showed that he had no regard at all for the rules of the road and he simply should not have been driving at all.

The starting point would therefore have been eight years' imprisonment with a range of 7 to 14 years, but it was considered that the chosen starting point was too high. The sentence was reduced to a starting point of 10 years leading to a sentence of eight-and-a-half years after 15% credit for guilty plea.

The Court also quashed the order for the defendant to take an extended driving test as he was already subject to such a requirement from his previous offence and s.36(7) of the Road Traffic Offenders Act 1988 makes it clear that such an order cannot be made if he is already subject to such an order.

Sentencing: causing serious injury by dangerous driving

In *R. v Brown*; *R. v Castano-Perez* [2021] EWCA Crim 1963, the two defend-   **5-208**
ants appealed against their sentences in respect of eight offences of causing serious injury by dangerous driving and 11 offences of causing bodily harm by wanton or furious driving. Brown was sentenced to a total of five years' imprisonment, and Castano-Perez to a total of four years and eight months due to an earlier plea.

Both had been to a car meet and had been driving their high-performance cars with a crowd of onlookers. The two cars collided and ploughed into the crowd injuring 19 people, eight of them seriously. In interview, both denied driving dangerously. In sentencing the judge referred to the context of the offences and that participants in cruise meets are generally young men who bring high performance cars, some of which are modified to further enhance their power. This was a toxic and dangerous combination. This was not an official or organised meeting and it had not been monitored by appropriate authorities for compliance with safety standards and a stretch of road was used as a form of racetrack. Such meets are dangerous, idiotic and run the risk that people will die or be injured every time they occur.

Both were young men in their early 20s and the judge took guidance from the death by dangerous driving guidelines. Had there been fatalities, this would have been level two as they had been driving at excessive speed with racing or competitive driving. The starting point was therefore five years with a range of four to seven years. A starting point of six years was used although this was beyond the maximum sentence for a single offence. Reference was made to *R. v Jenkins* [2015] EWCA Crim 105; [2015] 1 Cr. App. R. (S.) 70 (covered in this paragraph of the main work) highlighting that consecutive sentences should not be passed as it was a single act of dangerous driving. The sentencing guidelines in their definitive guidance on "Offences taken into consideration and totality" gives examples of where concurrent sentences should be passed. It states that where there is a single incident of dangerous driving resulting in injuries to multiple victims where there are separate charges relating to each victim, that the sentences should generally be passed concurrently, but each sentence should be aggravated to take into account the harm caused. See *https://www.sentencingcouncil.org.uk*.

In this case the judge had set the starting point above the statutory maximum which was an improper approach. The sentences were therefore reduced to three years and three months for Brown and three years for Castano-Perez.

In *R. v Harris* [2022] EWCA Crim 722, the defendant appealed against a sentence of four years' imprisonment on each of two counts of causing serious injury by dangerous driving. There were also two counts of drug driving, together with no insurance and no licence.

The defendant had overtaken an HGV and then hit a kerb with his vehicle going up in the air and the rear seat passenger ejected from the car and was found underneath it. The front seat passenger was also injured although his injuries were not as serious as those suffered by the female rear seat passenger. The driver did not have a licence or insurance and was found to have five times the legal limit of cocaine in his system and three times the legal limit for ketamine.

The appeal against the sentence was dismissed, although some useful comments were made about consecutive sentences as the sentencing judge had made reference to a starting point using consecutive sentences. That was clearly an error as the Sentencing Council guideline makes it clear, following the case of *R. v Jenkins* [2015] EWCA Crim 105; [2015] 1 Cr. App. R. (S.) 70 (as discussed above and in para.5-208 of the main work), that concurrent sentences will ordinarily be appropriate where a single incident of dangerous driving results in multiple victims.

The judge here would have been entitled to use a starting point at or near the maximum sentence of five years and after applying a 25% discount for the plea and taking account of the defendant's own injuries, would have led to a sentence of 40 to 45 months. Having taken account of totality including the drugs offences a total sentence of 48 months could be fully justified.

In *R. v White* [2022] EWCA Crim 599, there was an appeal against a sentence of 22 months' imprisonment on two counts of causing serious injury by dangerous driving.

The defendant had pursued thieves who had stolen motorcross bikes from his garage. He got in his high-powered Mercedes and followed the bikes in a two-mile chase along dark country roads. At one point he got so close to the bikes that a pillion passenger could turn around and strike the bonnet of the car with bolt cutters.

The defendant eventually lost control of his car and collided with the back of one of the bikes which then in turn collided with a parked car.

Both on the bike suffered serious injuries with the first suffering life threatening injuries with all his ribs broken, a fractured shoulder blade and a collapsed right lung, and the second a fractured skull, a bleed on the brain and right tibia fractured.

In sentencing the defendant, who was 30 and had no previous convictions, the judge observed that this was not a spur of the moment situation. It may have been in terms of getting in the car, but there was a pursuit of two miles when there was time to reflect and decide that this was not the right thing to do and he needed to drop back, turn around, go home, and call the police.

The two injured parties were on the same motorcycle and the passenger was not wearing a helmet, something that must have been apparent.

Appropriately using the *Causing death by dangerous driving* guideline to identify the level of seriousness, the judge concluded that the offending fell within level 1 as it was driving that involved a deliberate decision to ignore the rules of the road and an apparent disregard for the great danger being caused to others. Driving within two or three feet of a motor cyclist was clearly going to cause some risk to them when they are trying to evade you.

The appeal court concluded that the judge had been correct to place the offence in level one of the causing death by dangerous driving guidelines. The starting point of 30 months could not be criticised and a significant reduction had been allowed to reflect personal mitigation. 22 months was not manifestly excessive, and there could be not criticism in not suspending as the judge had considered this and stated:

"if you take the law into your own hands and if you drive in the manner that you did and put other people at risk of serious injury and cause serious injury to others by your driving, only an immediate custodial sentence is appropriate".

In *R. v Chism* [2022] EWCA Crim 637, the issue involved an appeal against a sentence of two years' detention in a young offenders' institution for an offence of causing serious injury by dangerous driving.

The defendant was 18 at the time of the commission of the offence and 19 when sentenced. Her mother had bought her an old Ford Fiesta for £850 and a couple of days later the defendant drove it without a licence or insurance.

She drove very fast and ignored pleas from her passengers to slow down. Her driving remained erratic and she eventually took a bend at speed, lost control and the vehicle turned over and ended up in a ditch.

One passenger, a Miss Witte, was flung from the car and she was found lying on her back in a field a good distance away from the car.

In sentencing, the judge stated that this was a very serious offence of its type because of the aggravating features, because she should not have been driving at all, and because of the continued dangerous driving over a considerable period of time. Not only was the custody threshold passed, but the only way of dealing with it was immediate custody.

On appeal the sentence was reduced to 18 months' detention in a young offenders' institution have taken into account the guidelines on sentencing young offenders, her age at the time, and that she had no previous convictions, this being her first experience of custody.

Dangerous and careless driving

5-244   In *R. v Kinzett* [2021] EWCA Crim 1938, the defendant appealed against his sentence of 12 months in a young offenders institution for an offence of dangerous driving.

He had been pursued in his Vauxhall Astra by the police and travelled across a park area where children were present. There was some issue about whether children had to jump out of the way of the car although the simple risk created was enough for sentencing. He had driven away from the police in order to evade capture due to the fact he had cannabis on him. He had several previous convictions and was subject to a current community order for an offensive weapon and drugs offences.

The starting point was considered to be 18 months' custody, and, with reduction for guilty plea, this was reduced to 12 months. The Court of Appeal considered this to be an appropriate sentence and the only issue left for the appeal was whether it should have been suspended. This was rejected in that the offence involved deliberate driving across a park with the presence of children and the judge was entitled to conclude that the appropriate punishment was one of immediate custody.

In *R. v Spencer* [2021] EWCA Crim 1901, there was again an appeal against sentence in a case of dangerous driving.

The defendant had been driving his Peugeot motor vehicle, had lost control on a roundabout and collided head on with a BMW. The passengers in the BMW all suffered minor injuries and their car was written off. The defendant and his passenger fled the scene and, in his trial, the defendant denied being the driver. CCTV and DNA evidence proved otherwise, and he was convicted at trial. He was also driving whilst disqualified and subject to a suspended sentence for a previous offence of dangerous driving.

The suspended sentence was activated as six months' imprisonment, together with 12 months for the offence of dangerous driving and four months consecutive for the offence of driving whilst disqualified, making a total sentence of 22 months. The Court of Appeal confirmed that 16 months for the new offences was both just and proportionate and the consecutive activation of the suspended sentence could not be criticised. The only corrections therefore on appeal were to remove the disqualification until a test was passed as the defendant was still subject to such an order from his previous offence of dangerous driving, and s.36(7) of the Road Traffic Offenders Act 1988 makes clear that the court may not make a further such order whilst he is so disqualified (see para.5-196 of the main work).

In *R. v Ashar* [2022] EWCA Crim 60, the defendant was sentenced to 12 months' imprisonment for an offence of dangerous driving, with two months consecutive for an offence of driving whilst disqualified. He also received a sentence of 14 days' imprisonment to be served concurrently for a separate offence of drug driving. He was disqualified for a total of five years and seven months and ordered to complete an extended driving test.

On 23 November 2020 he had been arrested for the offence of drug driving with a cannabis level of 3.3 micrograms per litre of blood, with the legal limit being 2. He received a postal requisition to appear at court on the 9 June 2021.

On the 16 April 2021, he failed to stop when seen by police driving an Astra and a pursuit ensued which lasted for some 20 minutes. He exceeded 70 mph in residential streets, overtook other cars and drove through several red lights. At one point he stopped to let a passenger out, but then continued and the pursuit only ended when the police deployed a stinger device.

It was then discovered that he was a disqualified driver, although otherwise was of good character.

In sentencing, the Recorder placed the offending in category 1, high culpability, and noted his recent disqualification. It was greater harm in view of the distance he covered and the bad driving. The starting point was 12 weeks with a range up to 26 weeks. She considered totality in sentencing for all matters and had considered whether to suspend. She reached a starting point of 18 months, reduced to 12 for the guilty plea and a consecutive three months reduced to two, for the driving whilst disqualified. Fourteen days was imposed for the drug driving.

The Appeal court said that the sentence was manifestly excessive for a young man with no previous convictions and reduced the starting point to nine months which, with credit for guilty plea, would be a sentence of 24 weeks for the dangerous driving. They did not interfere with the sentence for the driving whilst disqualified other than stating that it should have been concurrent as it arose out of the same facts.

The court did not consider whether suspension was appropriate as he had already served the equivalent of a six-month sentence. The disqualification was reduced to two years with an uplift of half the custodial term, namely 12 weeks.

CHAPTER 6

DRIVER OFFENCES

SPEED LIMITS: PROCEEDINGS AND PENALTIES

Fixed penalties and penalty points for speeding

6-152   Section 89 of the Police, Crime, Sentencing and Courts Act 2022 deals with courses as an alternative to prosecution and inserts a new Pt 3B into the 1988 Offenders Act.

In particular, a new s.90G gives a power to charge fees in England and Wales. It provides that the Chief Constable may charge a fee for enrolment on an approved course as an alternative to prosecution for a specified fixed penalty offence.

The legislation details that fees may be set that exceed the cost of an approved course, but that any excess must be used for the purpose of promoting road safety. A power is given to the Secretary of State to make regulations about the calculation, level, and use of fee income.

A new s.90H gives a power to prevent courses being offered to repeat offenders and again gives power to make regulations in that regard.

OBSTRUCTION, PARKING, ETC.: PENALTIES

Obstruction, parking, etc.: penalties

6-278   Section 80 of the Police, Crime, Sentencing and Courts Act 2022 makes a significant change to the sentencing powers for the offence under s.137 of the Highways Act 1980 of obstruction of the highway.

The offence previously carried a level 3 fine as the maximum punishment but, for offences committed on or after 12 May 2022, the offence now has a maximum penalty of a level 3 fine and/or 51 weeks' imprisonment.

Removal of illegally parked and abandoned vehicles

Section 90 of the Police, Crime, Sentencing and Courts Act 2022 amends s.102 **6-279**
of the Road Traffic Regulation Act 1984 and provides a statutory legal basis to
charge for vehicle recovery, storage and disposal, replacing a power inadvertently
removed in amendments made to the 1984 Act.

VEHICLE OFFENCES

TYPE APPROVAL SYSTEM

Vehicles subject to type approval

8-09   From 6 July 2022, under the EU General Safety Regulations (Regulation (EU) No.2019/2144) (GSR) new motor vehicles made for the EU market will have to be equipped with advanced safety systems to reduce the number of fatalities and severe injuries on EU roads. Following an agreement with the European Parliament, the European Council adopted a regulation on the general safety of motor vehicles and the protection of vehicle occupants and vulnerable road users such as pedestrians and cyclists. Under the new rules motor vehicles will have to be equipped with safety features including intelligent speed assistance, alcohol interlock installation facilitation, driver drowsiness and attention warning systems, advanced driver distraction warning systems and event data recorders. Motor vehicles will also be required to include enlarged head impact protection zones capable of mitigating injuries in the event of a collision for vulnerable users such as cyclists and pedestrians. The UK has exited from the EU so is not bound to implement these new provisions. The safety measures are covered by international agreements through the United Nations.

The Department for Transport is working to deliver a full scheme which is expected to become mandatory in spring 2023. Once this is in place, and subject to having sufficient powers to amend retained EU legislation, the Department will be able to make amendments to the requirements for vehicles registered in GB. Any changes to the mandatory requirements for vehicle approval in GB, including elements of the GSR, will be subject to the standard consultation protocols and the availability of parliamentary time. The technical requirements for new vehicle regulations are generally developed at an international level by the United Nations Economic Commission for Europe (UNECE) and the UK is an active participant in this work. Although the Government has made no decision yet as to which technologies from the GSR might form part of the national vehicle approval requirements, the Department remains a member of the European New Car

Assessment Programme (Euro NCAP). Euro NCAP is an independent, not-for-profit, organisation that provides motorists with objective information on the crash safety of cars. The 1–5 star rating system helps consumers compare the safety potential of different models, helping to include safety in their purchasing decision. In turn, this provides market incentive to drive delivery of innovative road safety solutions into the vehicle fleet far quicker than regulations alone. The car rating programme already incentivises many of the technologies called up in the GSR.

SPECIFIC CONSTRUCTION AND USE REGULATIONS

Rear markings

The Road Vehicles (Display of Registration Marks) (Amendment) (EU Exit) (No.2) Regulations 2020 (SI 2020/1363) prohibited the fitting of GB registration plates with the EU symbol from 1 January 2021. Any GB EU registration plates fitted before 1 January 2021 may remain displayed. The union flag, flag of St George, the red dragon of Wales and the cross of St Andrew can be displayed on the left-hand side of the registration plate. From 21 September 2021, UK-registered vehicles used in the EU must be marked with a UK sticker (not a GB sticker) displayed clearly on the rear of the vehicle unless the registration plate has a clear UK mark on it, including the union flag. If the registration plate has a union flag with a GB marker then there has to be a UK sticker in addition. The same applies if the rear registration plate has a Euro symbol or a national flag of England, Scotland or Wales or no symbol—only the registration number. In Spain, Cyprus or Malta there has to be a UK sticker regardless of what is on the rear registration plate. There is no requirement for a UK sticker if driving in Ireland. **8-27**

Tyres

The Road Vehicles (Construction and Use) (Amendment) Regulations 2020 (SI 2020/1178) came into force on 1 February 2021. They amend the Road Vehicles (Construction and Use) Regulations 1986 (SI 1986/1078) making provision about the age of tyres (including re-treaded tyres), and the legibility of date markings on tyres, which are permitted for use on buses (including minibuses) and goods vehicles with a maximum gross weight exceeding 3,500kg. It also amends Table 2 of Sch.2 to the 1986 Regulations to include the provisions about re-treaded tyres in ECE Regulations 108 and 109. **8-56**

Silencers, noise and warning instruments

On 14 July 2021 the Department for Transport published "Transitioning to zero emissions cars and vans: 2035 delivery plan" outlining its plans to increase the use of electric vehicles and to introduce a new road vehicles CO_2 regulatory emission regime in 2024. As part of this transition, EU Regulation No.540/2014 requires manufacturers to fit an Acoustic Vehicle Alerting System (AVAS) to all new types of quiet electric or hybrid vehicles from 1 July 2019. The AVAS must emit a noise if the vehicle is travelling at below 20 kph or 12 mph. Since the agreement to fix AVAS is based on an international agreement which the UK remains party to, it is unlikely to be affected by the UK withdrawal from the EU. The EU Regulation allowed manufacturers to install a pause switch for the AVAS to allow drivers to **8-70** temporarily disable it. Following objections, it was agreed in 2019 to remove this provision. Manufacturers have been given to 2023 to make adjustments.

Mobile telephones

8-77   As noted in the main work, in January 2021 the Government consulted about changing the law on the use of mobile phones while driving as a result of the decision in *DPP v Barreto* [2019] EWHC 2044 (Admin); [2020] 1 W.L.R. 599. The Government published its response in September 2021 stating that it proposes to amend the law so that the offence of using a hand-held mobile phone while driving captures drivers who are using their phone for "standalone" functions as well as those using interactive communication functions. The Government noted some of the misunderstandings and requests for clarification which were received in response to this proposal (for example, relating to the use of satnavs on phones and whether the stop phase of stop-start engines allows a driver lawfully to use a hand-held mobile phone) and plans to deal with them through expanded guidance. The list of prohibited functions will take account of some of the suggestions made by consultees. A majority of consultees requested an exemption for contactless payment by mobile phone. The Government proposals state that it intends to clarify that the contactless payment exemption will apply solely where a contactless payment is made by tapping on a card reader; the exemption will not apply where drivers make an internet payment whilst sitting at the wheel with the engine running. Rule 149 of the revised Highway Code (issued on 29 January 2022) states that using hands free equipment is likely to distract a driver's attention from the road. Rule 149 goes on to advise that it is far safer not to use any telephone while driving or riding and that drivers or riders should find a safe place to stop first or use the voicemail facility and listen to messages later.

The Government amended reg.110 of the Road Vehicles (Construction and Use) Regulations 1986 (SI 1986/1078) for offences committed on or after 25 March 2022 so that in addition to using a mobile phone for interactive communication, it is now an offence to use a hand-held mobile phone to: illuminate the screen; check the time; check notifications; unlock the device; make, receive or reject a telephone or internet based call; send, receive or upload oral or written content; send, receive or upload a photo or video; utilise camera, video, or sound recording functionality; draft any text; access any stored data such as documents, books, audio files, photos, videos, films, playlists, notes or messages; access an application; access the internet. There are exceptions. A mobile phone may be used legally: in an emergency, to make a contactless payment for goods or services provided there and then (e.g. toll road or drive-through), but only if the vehicle is stationary, or as a satnav, provided it is kept in a cradle, not held in the hand.

For offences committed before 25 March 2022, the case of *Bendt v CPS* [2022] EWHC 502 (Admin) considered the case of a driver using his mobile phone whilst driving in order to change the music he was listening to played through the car's sound system. The High Court was not asked to go behind *DPP v Barreto*. The High Court ruled that reg.110(6)(c) did not require communication to be with or from anyone and could involve communication with another device. The driver was rightly convicted under reg.110 because he was using his phone while driving to interactively communicate with another device rather than simply using an internal phone function as covered by *DPP v Barreto*.

CHAPTER 9

PROTECTION OF DRIVERS AND PASSENGERS

GENERALLY

Seat belt reminder systems were made compulsory for the driver seat in all new **9-01** passenger cars from 2014 through Regulation (EC) 661/2009 in compliance with United Nations (UN) Regulations. This requirement for a seat belt reminder system for all front and rear seats came into force in the EU for all new motor vehicles from 1 September 2021. Since this was in response to amendments to UN Regulations, the legal position in England and Wales is not affected by the exit from the EU.

MOTOR CYCLE HELMETS

Wearing of helmets

The Government considered the mandatory use of cycle helmets in detail as part **9-56** of its "Cycling and Walking Investment Strategy safety review" in 2018 but decided against this and continues to recommend usage of cycle helmets. For e-scooters local authorities trialling their use can include provision about the wearing of helmets or availability at the point of hire in their agreement(s) with operators.

INSURANCE

Third Party Insurance Policies

Generally

10-02 For insurance purposes an e-scooter is a "motor vehicle" (see para.1-38 in the main work) and so must have motor insurance. If the e-scooter is rented, insurance is likely to be provided by the rental operator.

The Motor Insurers' Bureau

10-12 The main work refers to the decision in *Colley v Shuker* [2020] EWHC 3433 (QB); [2021] R.T.R. 17 in which it was confirmed that the obligation on the MIB extended to situations where the vehicle was insured but the law of the Member State allowed the insurer to avoid liability thus leaving a third party without a remedy. The MIB's appeal against this decision has been dismissed: *Colley v MIB* [2022] EWCA Civ 360; [2022] R.T.R. 19. Avoidance of a policy by an insurer for material misrepresentation was not permitted under art.3 of Directive 2009/103 and so the MIB, as an emanation of the State, has to compensate the claimant. Whether such provisions can legitimately be included in a policy is for the national law to resolve but this does not affect the obligations of the MIB which were governed by arts 3 and 10 which were of direct effect.

Green Card system

10-17 Though the UK lost membership of the Green Card Free Circulation Zone (GCFCZ) following withdrawal from the EU, the EU reinstated that membership by making the UK a third party country. UK drivers do not need an insurance green card when travelling in a GCFCZ country which includes EU countries, Albania, Azerbaijan, Belarus, Moldova, Russia, Turkey and the Ukraine.

DRIVING LICENCES

PROVISIONS AND OFFENCES

Generally

On 5 August 2022 the Government published an open consultation entitled **11-02** "Driving licensing call for evidence". The document contains suggestions for extending driving licence entitlement. For further details, please see Ch.13 (below).

With regard to the requirement to specify the type of vehicles which are used for **11-08** a driving test, the Motor Vehicles (Driving Licences) (Amendment) Regulations 2022 (SI 2022/110) amend the 1999 Regulations and make provision for changes to the specification requirements for category A2 motorcycles used for practical driving tests, and the upgrading of entitlements where a second driving test is passed in an automatic transmission vehicle. The amendments came into force on 1 March 2022.

Production of licences

If a driver fails to renew a photocard licence and fails to surrender it after the **11-22** photograph has expired, an offence is committed under s.99(5) of the 1988 Act. The offence is one of failing to comply with the duty to surrender the photocard licence not less than every 10 years (s.99(2A) of the 1988 Act). A failure to surrender this licence does not invalidate the driving licence itself which continues in force until its expiry date or some other event such as revocation or disqualification by a court. No offence under s.87(1) of the 1988 Act is committed.

DRIVING WHILE DISQUALIFIED

The offence (s.103)

In order to clarify the effect of s.102A of the Road Traffic Act 1988, which sets **11-81** out the effect of a disqualification imposed by a court in Northern Ireland, the Isle of Man, the Channel Islands and Gibraltar in terms of its recognition in Great Britain, it should be noted that whilst a disqualification imposed in one of the above territories is recognised in Great Britain, an offence of driving while disqualified is not committed in Great Britain. A person who is disqualified as described above will not be entitled to drive because that person is not able to apply for a licence in

Great Britain by virtue of s.102 of the 1988 Act. Such a person, is, therefore, disqualified for the purposes of preventing an application being made for a licence or obtaining a licence.

CHAPTER 12

EXCISE AND TRADE LICENCES

TABLE OF CONTENTS

TRADE LICENCES

Display of trade plates

The requirement for the licence-holder of a trade licence to fix the trade licence **12-112** to a trade plate was removed by virtue of the Vehicle Excise and Registration (Consequential Amendments) Regulations 2014 (SI 2014/2358).

GOODS AND PASSENGER VEHICLES

TABLE OF CONTENTS

DRIVER LICENSING: LARGE GOODS VEHICLES, HEAVY GOODS VEHICLES,
PASSENGER-CARRYING VEHICLES AND PUBLIC SERVICE VEHICLES

LGV and PCV drivers' licences

13-02   The open consultation document "Driving licensing call for evidence", published on 5 August 2022, contains specific suggestions concerning the extension of the licensing entitlement of drivers who hold a car (category B) licence entitlement. The suggestion is to grant such drivers additional entitlement to an HGV (category C1) licence and to a minibus (category D1) licence. Both suggestions have road safety implications and the consultation is designed to seek views from all interested parties. The consultation closes on 28 October 2022 and the full text of the document can be found at *https://www.gov.uk/government/consultations/driving-licensing-review-call-for-evidence-on-opportunities-for-changes-to-the-driver-licensing-regime* [Accessed 20 September 2022].

13-05   Further amendments to the Motor Vehicles (Driving Licences) Regulations 1999 (SI 1999/2864) were introduced with effect from 15 November 2021 by the Motor Vehicles (Driving Licences) (Amendment) (No.4) Regulations 2021 (SI 2021/1251).They remove some of the existing requirements for "staging" in the process of achieving an articulated heavy goods vehicle licence (category C+E) or a heavy trailer drawing passenger carrying vehicle licence (category D+E).

Goods Vehicle Operators' Licences

Generally

The traffic commissioners for Great Britain published an updated Goods Vehicle **13-35** Operator Licensing Guide on 14 July 2022. The Guide is an overview of how the operator licensing system works for operators of goods vehicles. It is intended to give a summary of operator licensing and to direct users where further advice may be available. Clarification is provided in respect of modern rules and regulations and adheres to current accessibility criteria. Details are included of the requirements for operator licensing, how to apply for a licence, managing a licence and the role and responsibilities of transport managers. The guide can be found at *https://www.gov.uk/ guidance/goods-vehicle-operator-licensing-guide* [Accessed 20 September 2022].

Types of operator's licence

Standard operator's licence

It should be noted that with effect from 21 May 2022, the UK became obliged **13-37** to licence a person who carries goods vehicles to the EU for hire or reward using a goods vehicle exceeding 2.5 tonnes in mass when laden. At the time of writing, under both the laws of England and Wales and Scotland and Northern Ireland, a person is required to hold a licence for such a carriage only if the goods vehicle exceeds 3.5 tonnes in mass when laden. The Goods Vehicles (Licensing of Operators) (Amendment) Regulations 2022 (SI 2022/293) make the necessary amendments to meet the obligation of the UK under Title I of Heading Three of Part Two of the Trade and Co-operation Agreement between the United Kingdom of the one part and the European Union and the European Atomic Energy Community, of the other part (Treaty Series No. 8 (2021), "the TCA"). After the commencement of the Regulations, pre-existing operator's licence became a heavy goods vehicle licence and may be varied (an application to authorise one or more light goods vehicles, for example, if it does not already authorise a sufficient number of goods vehicles).

A light goods vehicle licence is available to any person who uses only light goods vehicles for the carriage of goods. A standard international light goods vehicle licence is sufficient for a person who is obliged after 11 pm on 20 May 2022 to hold an operator's licence to hold a light goods vehicle licence (of any type) for any other reason.

Consequential amendments are also made to Regulation (EC) No.1071/2009 and Regulation (EC) No.1072/2009.

PSV Licensing and Fitness Requirements

Offences

Cases

The powers of traffic commissioners extend to the disqualification of operators **13-204** if an operator's licence is revoked. In *Coach Hire Surrey Ltd v Traffic Commissioner for London and South East Traffic Area* [2020] EWCA Civ 1706; [2021] R.T.R. 20 the Court of Appeal held that a 10-year disqualification period imposed under the Public Passenger Vehicles Act 1981 Pt II ss.17(3)(c) and 14ZA(3)(a) was justified in the case of a transport manager who had failed to disclose relevant convictions on his application for an operator's licence. In determining the length of the disqualification period, traffic commissioners were not constrained by any tariff system but should have regard to the "guidance" section in Statutory Document No.10, entitled "The Principles of Decision Making and the Concept of Proportionality".

CHAPTER 15

THEFT, TAKING CONVEYANCES, AGGRAVATED VEHICLE-TAKING, CRIMINAL DAMAGE AND CAUSING DANGER TO ROAD USERS

TABLE OF CONTENTS

AGGRAVATED VEHICLE-TAKING: PROCEEDINGS AND PENALTIES

Sentencing guidelines

It is wrong to suggest that persons who allow themselves to be carried in vehicles **15-40** taken by others are to be regarded as no more culpable than those who commit a basic offence when convicted of aggravated offences. Section 12A of the Theft Act 1968 makes a person who is guilty of the basic offence strictly liable for the aggravating behaviour of the driver by treating the passenger as having control of the vehicle (see *R. v Taylor* [2016] UKSC 5: [2016] R.T.R. 28 at [28]). The mere absence of evidence to show encouragement does not absolve the passenger of culpability, which is likely to be the most significant factor when considering sentencing a passenger (see *R. v Woolley* [2005] EWCA Crim 2853; [2006] 1 Cr. App. R. (S.) 123). Furthermore, a court is entitled to conclude it necessary to disqualify passengers until they pass an extended driving test, for the protection of the public, when they have shown reckless disregard for any rules relating to the driving of cars—*R. v Wilson* [2022] EWCA Crim 807; [2022] Crim. L.R. 853. Wilson had consumed alcohol and cocaine with the driver who had travelled at over twice the 30 mph speed limit, failed to stop at a red light, narrowly missed three workmen and collided with a boy walking on the pavement who later died in hospital. Wilson had a bad driving record and a previous conviction for supplying drugs. He was convicted after trial though and he pleaded guilty to an offence of supplying cocaine. The driver was sentenced to nine years' imprisonment for the offence of causing death by dangerous driving, the appellant passenger was sentenced to three years for aggravated vehicle taking and three years and four months consecutively for the drugs offence. He was disqualified for 98 months and until he passed an extended test. His appeal against the sentence imposed for the vehicle taking offence was dismissed.

CUSTODIAL AND OTHER PENALTIES

INTRODUCTION

The legislative framework

18-01   The Criminal Procedure Rules 2020 (SI 2020/759) have been further amended. The effect of the Criminal Procedure (Amendment No.2) Rules 2021 (SI 2021/849) is that r.3.16 now makes provision regarding the opportunity for a defendant to ask the court for an indication of whether a custodial or non-custodial sentence is more likely in the event of a guilty plea there and then.

The Magistrates' Court Sentencing Guidelines

18-05   There have been some, relatively minor, changes to the explanatory material that supports these guidelines. In relation to the approach where considering whether or not to disqualify a defendant who is not present, the relevant guidance now states:

> "When considering disqualification in absence the starting point should be that disqualification in absence should be imposed if there is no reason to believe the defendant is not aware of the proceedings, and after the statutory notice has been served pursuant to section 11(4) of the Magistrates' Courts Act 1980 where appropriate. Disqualification should not be imposed in absence where there is evidence that the defendant has an acceptable reason for not attending or where there are reasons to believe it would be contrary to the interests of justice to do so."

The Sentencing Council is (at the time of writing) consulting on a range of miscellaneous amendments to guidelines which includes this wording. The closing date for responses to the consultation is 30 November 2022: *https://www.sentencingcouncil.org.uk/publications/item/miscellaneous-amendments-to-sentencing-guidelines-consultation-2022/* [Accessed 22 September 2022].

FINES

The assessment and imposition of fines

In relation to offences committed on or after 16 June 2022, the amounts pay- **18-11** able in relation to the criminal justice surcharge have increased as a result of the Sentencing Act 2020 (Surcharge) (Amendment) Regulations 2022 (SI 2022/584).

The table below shows the amounts effective in relation to offences committed on or after 14 April 2020 (as set out in the main work) and those which apply to offences committed on or after 16 June 2022. See the main work for the approach where there are mixed disposals or the defendant is being sentenced for offences that occurred at times when the rates were different.

	14 April 2020-15 June 2022	16 June 2022 onwards
	£17	£20
	£22	£26
	£34	£41
	£95	£114
	£128	£154
	£156	£187
	£190	£228
Fine	10% (no less than £34, no more than £190)	40% (maximum £2,000)

IMPRISONMENT AND OTHER CUSTODIAL SENTENCES

Statutory restrictions on imposition of discretionary custodial sentences

For either-way offences committed on or after 2 May 2022, the maximum **18-16** sentence able to be imposed by a magistrates' court has been increased from six months to 12 months. See the Criminal Justice Act 2003 (Commencement No.33) and Sentencing Act 2020 (Commencement No.2) Regulations 2022 (SI 2022/500) and the Criminal Justice Act 2003 (Commencement No.34) and Judicial Review and Courts Act 2022 (Commencement No.1) Regulations 2022 (SI 2022/816).

ENDORSEMENT AND PENALTY POINTS

TABLE OF CONTENTS

PROCEDURE ON CONVICTION

Production of driving licence

19-37   Section 91 of the Police, Crime, Sentencing and Courts Act 2022 (which was not in force at the time of writing, September 2022) will remove the requirement for a person to produce their driving licence when prosecuted or dealt with for an offence involving obligatory endorsement. Section 7 of the 1988 Offenders Act will be amended to reflect the fact that penalty points and endorsements are recorded electronically on an offender's driving record. The amended provisions will still require a person to bring their licence to court if they attend for an offence which carries obligatory or discretionary disqualification. They also allow courts to require an offender to produce their licence once convicted when considering disqualifying the offender from driving. In reality courts now seldom require offenders to surrender their licences at the court hearing; s.97 of the 2022 Act will, when in force, introduce s.37A to the Offenders Act allowing the Secretary of State (through the DVLA) to require a person who has been disqualified to surrender their licence. A person who, without a reasonable excuse, fails to do so will be liable to a level 3 fine. Similar provisions contained in s.95 of the 2022 Act will, when in force, apply in respect of new drivers whose licences are revoked because they incur six or more penalty points: they too could be required to surrender their licence. By virtue of s.37(1A) which was added by the Road Traffic Act 1991, the driving licence of an offender who is disqualified for shorter than 56 days may be treated as becoming valid again at the end of the disqualification period. The purpose of this legislation was to remove the need for those offenders to surrender their licences and obviate the need to reapply at the end of their disqualification period. The Act, it appears will leave this provision unaltered, presumably the Secretary of State will only seek surrender of licences where the holder is:

- disqualified for period is 56 days or longer,
- disqualified pending passing of a driving test, or
- a new driver whose licence is revoked.

The main work notes at paras 20-62 and 20-70 that the 2020 Sentencing Code does not require an offender to produce their licence when the court disqualifies them for an offence pursuant to ss.163 (disqualification for any offence) or 164 (where vehicle used for purposes of crime). This appeared to be an oversight as ss.146 and 147 of the Powers of Criminal Courts (Sentencing) Act 2000 contained such a requirement and the Code was intended only to codify the existing provisions. The Act fills this lacuna by allowing the Secretary of State to require production of a licence held by "a person who ... is disqualified by an order of a court" under what becomes s.37A of the 1988 Offenders Act which is inserted by s.92 of the 2022 Act, but is not in force at the time of writing (September 2022). As this section applies to anyone who "is disqualified by an order of a court", it appears to apply to disqualifications imposed under the 2020 Sentencing Code and not just to those imposed under the 1988 Offenders Act.

CHAPTER 20

DISQUALIFICATION

GENERAL PRINCIPLES

Period and commencement of disqualification

Length

20-20   It is helpful if courts briefly explain the rationale for the period of any disqualification they impose in accordance with the guidance in *R. v Needham* [2016] EWCA Crim 455; [2016] R.T.R. 23 at [48]. The Court of Appeal reduced a three-year disqualification to one of 18 months (comprising of a 16 months discretionary period and two month extension under s.166 of the Sentencing Code) in the case of an 18-year-old who had pleaded guilty to a prolonged period of dangerous driving. The driving, which included unsuccessfully attempting a handbrake turn, reversing for 20 metres, driving at speed over speed bumps, causing a tailback by slowing excessively, driving at over 100 mph and racing with a vehicle that overtook him and then hitting a roundabout causing the car to fly into the air and lodge itself in the side of a building. He persisted despite his passengers, who were not badly injured, warning him about his driving. He was fortunate not to have seriously injured or killed someone. The sentencing judge had recognised the offender was young, had pleaded guilty and was of positively good character. At the time of the offence he was in full-time employment at a supermarket and he had intended to apply to join the Police having been a Police Cadet, he had won awards for his community engagement and for bravery when attending a road rage incident when he pacified the parties. He also assisted in the care of a younger brother who suffered from attention deficit hyperactivity disorder. The Court of Appeal took account of the principles articulated in *R. v Backhouse* [2010] EWCA Crim 1111: that disqualification is intended to punish and deter, it also has the purpose of protecting the public from harm, and that a balance has to be struck such that the court ought not to disqualify for a period that is longer than is necessary. Bearing in mind the effect of a ban on employment prospects and the like, whilst not condoning the defendant's driving, the period of the disqualification would accordingly be reduced—*R. v Playfair* [2021] EWCA Crim 644; [2022] 1 Cr. App. R. (S.) 4.

Ten years' disqualification was not excessive in the case of a man who pleaded guilty to causing death by careless or inconsiderate driving when he drove a van, at 14 mph in a 20-mph zone, through a pedestrian-crossing red light which had been red for over four seconds. He hit a pedestrian on the crossing who later died from her injuries. He was genuinely remorseful, he was an ex-serviceman with post-traumatic stress disorder having been in a road traffic accident himself 20 years previously. He had previous convictions for driving with excess alcohol and for driving whilst disqualified. The judge was right to find greater culpability and that the appellant was a real and continuing danger to other road users. He had considered taking his own life previously by crashing his car and appeared to need psychiatric therapy. The disqualification period was appropriate in the light of those features and the authorities which suggest substantial disqualifications for such offences—*R. v Austin* [2020] EWCA Crim 1269; [2021] R.T.R. 21. The judge had borne in mind the consequences for the appellant and his wife, for whom he was the primary carer, including the fact that they lived in a rural area.

An appellant who was imprisoned for 12 months and disqualified for 10 years for his fourth offence of dangerous driving appealed against the disqualification. The dangerous driving took place over a short period. The appellant was told to stop by the police, appeared to do so then accelerated away and collided with a roundabout and another car; he then tried to reverse out having been blocked by police vehicles and rammed the other vehicle again. The occupants of the vehicle, who included a child, required hospital treatment. The Court of Appeal concluded a five-year disqualification with a six-month extension was sufficient, having regard to principles enumerated in *R. v Islam* [2019] EWCA Crim 1494 at [11]–[13], summarised as follows:

1. Disqualification should not be so long that it disproportionately adversely affects the prospects of rehabilitation. Regard should be had to the offender's individual circumstances and his prospects of rehabilitation and what is required to prevent harm to the public.
2. There is a punitive element in disqualification from driving. It is part of the sentence and the sentence should reflect culpability and harm and should achieve the statutory purpose of sentencing set out in (what was then) s.142 of the Criminal Justice Act 2003 which include punishment.
3. There is no formula by which a court can measure the right length of disqualification. It is a judicial decision which should produce a result tailored to the offender and to the offence.

Where the offender falls to be sentenced to a mandatory minimum disqualification, that minimum is not a starting point. A seven-year disqualification, together with an uplift for the period the offender would be in custody, was not manifestly excessive where the appellant pleaded guilty to two offences of causing serious injury whilst driving dangerously as well as offences which included disqualified driving, driving whilst unfit to drive through drink or drugs and failing to provide a specimen. The appellant, who was 20 years old at the time of the offences, had an appalling record which included previous convictions for dangerous driving and failing to provide a breath specimen. He was over twice the drink drive limit, tested positive for cocaine and cannabis when screened at the roadside and he was involved in a police chase. The Crown Court had miscalculated the uplift (which should have been longer) and, because the Court of Appeal could not increase the overall disqualification it reduced the discretionary part of the disqualification to give effect to that period announced by the judge at first instance—*R. v Morrison* [2021] EWCA Crim 917; [2022] 1 Cr. App. R. (S) 20.

Disqualification and custodial sentences

20-24   Sections 35A of the 1988 Offenders Act and 166(5) of the 2020 Sentencing Code, which detail the extension periods that Parliament has prescribed when courts impose disqualifications and immediate custodial sentences, have now been amended so they reflect the changes made by the Release of Prisoners (Alteration of Relevant Proportion of Sentence) Order 2020 (SI 2020/158). That order provides that offenders sentenced to seven years or more for violent or sexual offences will not be released on licence until they have served two-thirds of their sentence. This change rectifies the problem identified by the Court of Appeal in *R. v Long* [2020] EWCA Crim 1729; [2021] 4 W.L.R. 5. Sections 35A and 166 now provide that the relevant extension period shall be two-thirds of such a custodial sentence (previously the legislation specified the extension period to be half the sentence). The Counter-Terrorism and Sentencing Act 2021 also made similar alterations to extension periods for certain terrorist offences.

Section 166 of the Sentencing Code provides a table of the relevant periods which apply to disqualifications imposed under the Code. Although that section does not apply to disqualifications imposed under the 1988 Offenders Act, it accurately reflects the provision of s.35A of that Act. The list of relevant extension periods in the main work at § 20-24 should now read:

1. Detention and training order under s.233 (offenders under 18: detention and training orders): half the term of the order. [1]
2. Sentences of detention under s.252A (special sentence of detention for terrorist offenders of particular concern): two-thirds of the term imposed pursuant to s.252A(5) (the appropriate custodial term) unless s.247A(2A) of the Criminal Justice Act 2003 (restricted eligibility for release on licence of terrorist prisoners) applies, in which case it is the whole of the term. [1A]
3. Extended sentences of detention under s.254 (persons under 18): two-thirds of the term imposed pursuant to s.254(a) (the appropriate custodial term). [2]
4. Sentences under s.265 (special custodial sentence for certain offenders of particular concern: adults aged 18 to 20): two-thirds of the term imposed pursuant to s.265(2)(a) (the appropriate custodial term). [3]
5. Extended sentences of detention in a young offender institution: two-thirds of the term imposed pursuant to s.266(a) (the appropriate custodial term) unless s.247A(2A) of the Criminal Justice Act 2003 (restricted eligibility for release on licence of terrorist prisoners) applies, in which case it is the whole of the term. [4]
6. Serious terrorism sentences of detention in a young offender institution: the term imposed pursuant to s.268C(2) (the appropriate custodial term). [4A]
7. Sentences under s.278 (special custodial sentence for certain offenders of particular concern: adults aged 21 and over): two-thirds the term imposed pursuant to s.278(2)(a) (the appropriate custodial term). [5]
8. Extended sentences of imprisonment: two-thirds of the term imposed pursuant to s.279(a) (the appropriate custodial term) unless s.247A(2A) of the Criminal Justice Act 2003 (restricted eligibility for release on licence of terrorist prisoners) applies, in which case it is the whole of the term. [6]

9. Serious terrorism sentences of imprisonment: the term imposed pursuant to s.282C(2) (the appropriate custodial term). [6A]
10. Custodial sentences in respect of which s.244ZA of the Criminal Justice Act 2003 applies to the offender: two-thirds of the sentence. [6B]
11. Custodial sentences not within any of the preceding entries in respect of which s.247A of the Criminal Justice Act 2003 applies to the offender: two-thirds of the sentence. [6C]
12. Life sentences in relation to which a minimum term order is made under s.321(2): the term specified in the minimum term order. [7]
13. Any other case: half the custodial sentence imposed. [8]

The references in square brackets are to the numbered table included in s.166 of the Code.

OBLIGATORY DISQUALIFICATIONS

Obligatory disqualification

Where the Crown Court fails to impose an obligatory disqualification and later **20-33** purports to do so administratively, that disqualification is invalid. The judge failed to announce obligatory disqualifications when the appellants were sentenced, though did say their driving records would be endorsed. It appears the judge attempted to rectify the error when the omission was noticed. As the disqualification orders increased the appellants' overall sentences they should have been pronounced in open court on notice to the applicants in accordance with the Criminal Procedure Rules r.28.4(2)(b) and (4)). The Court of Appeal could not rectify the error as it could not impose a sentence that resulted in the appellant being treated more severely than at first instance—*R. v Turner*; *R. v Robinson* [2021] EWCA Crim 1376; [2022] R.T.R. 11.

Provisions of the Police, Crime, Sentencing and Courts Act 2022, which are now in force, make changes to the minimum periods of disqualification for certain offences.

1. The minimum period of disqualification for causing death by dangerous driving and causing death by careless driving when under the influence of drink or drugs is now five years (s.86(8)—which inserts subs.(4ZA) into s.34 of the 1988 Offenders Act).
2. The minimum disqualification for an offence of causing death by careless driving when under the influence of drink or drugs rises to six years if the offender has been convicted of the same offence in the 10 years preceding commission of the present offence.

DISCRETIONARY DISQUALIFICATIONS

Disqualification where vehicle used for crime

The main work notes that the Sentencing Code 2020 omits any requirement for **20-62** a person who is disqualified under ss.146 or 147 to produce their driving licence to the court. When in force, the Police, Crime, Sentencing and Courts Act 2022 will address this by empowering the Secretary of State to require its surrender—see further commentary in this supplement at para.19-37 above.

Disqualification for any offence or for the enforcement of fines

20-70   Whilst case law reported in the main work (e.g. *R. v Cliff* [2004] EWCA Crim 3139; [2005] 2 Cr. App. R. (S.) 118 and *R. v Sofekun* [2008] EWCA Crim 2035; [2009] 1 Cr. App. R. (S) 78) confirms that a plain reading of what is now s.163 of the Sentencing Code does not require a court to find any link between an offender's behaviour and disqualification, "ordinarily the court no doubt will look for some link between the criminality and the driving or use of a vehicle (see cases such as *Gilder* [2012] 1 Cr. App. R. (S) 4 and *Cliff* [above] ... and also as clarified and explained in *Griffin* [2019] 2 Cr. App. R. (S.) 33"—*R. v Bains* [2022] EWCA Crim 100 at [17]. In the earlier cases cited the Court of Appeal had upheld disqualifications where a motor vehicle was used in the commission of the crimes for which the appellants had been sentenced. In some of those cases cited, the court of first instance had not explained whether it had exercised its power to disqualify under what is now s.163 (disqualification for any offence) or s.164 (disqualification where vehicle used for purposes of crime) of the Code. Bains was convicted of doing acts tending and intended to pervert the course of public justice and disqualified for 12 months with an extension of four months to reflect the time he would be in custody. He and his wife had initially told the police she was driving at the time a man had died having been hit by a vehicle in the road. His wife was arrested under suspicion of causing death by dangerous driving. Mr Bains was investigated for the offence when evidence came to light that he was the driver. He then admitted driving, and told the police that he had hit something he thought was debris. He said he had stopped, discovered a lorry had run over the body panicked and left the scene—he was an HGV driver and feared losing his job. The sentencing judge accepted Bains was not responsible for the death but concluded he would have been prosecuted for failing to stop or report the accident had those offences not been time-barred. The appellant had "engaged in ... deception ... of the gravest kind, with the authorities and a family seeking the truth about the loss of a young and promising life". Whilst the Court of Appeal accepted the disqualification would have a significant impact on the appellant when he was released from custody, the court bore in mind "that disqualification from driving is not necessarily or even primarily a punitive element of a sentence, even though of course it plays a part in punishment"; however, it observed that "[v]ery important further aspects of the rationale for disqualifying from driving are both deterrence and the protection of the public" [17]. In the present case there was link between the offence and driving. The appellant who had been fined (albeit many years before) for offences of driving without due care and attention, failing to stop after an accident, failing to report an accident and using a car while uninsured appeared not to have learned his lesson. The fact he was an HGV driver was an aggravating, rather than mitigating, feature.

The Court of Appeal reached a different conclusion in another case where a driver of a vehicle was convicted of doing an act tending and intended to pervert the course of justice by falsely reporting that his car had been stolen. The appeal court found that the Crown Court had erred in disqualifying him. The driver's DNA was found on the vehicle's airbag after it had crashed into a building causing extensive damage. The driver had made off and an innocent man had been arrested and charged with aggravated vehicle taking—that man was only cleared once the forensic evidence showed the accused to be the driver. The Crown had not brought proceedings for failing to stop and failing to report an accident, even though such a prosecution was not time-barred by s.127 of the Magistrates' Courts Act 1980; a report of the forensic evidence was completed 12 days before that six-month time limit would have expired (the case does not say when the report was received by the Crown but concludes the Crown could have initiated summary proceedings). The appellant had been charged with dangerous driving but the Crown did not pursue that charge (presumably because it could not prove the requisite fault). The offender had a previous conviction in 1998 for driving with excess alcohol. Unsurprisingly, some might think, the judge at first instance concluded that the reason the offender made the false report of theft was to hide his involvement. She disqualified him for 16 months. The Court of Appeal considered the case of *R. v Cornell-Gallardo* [2010] EWCA Crim 3151 in which the appellant had been convicted of assaulting a cyclist who took exception to the manner of the offender's driving and the judge disqualified him. In that case the Court of Appeal had concluded "it was unnecessary to impose a disqualification from driving on the basis that this incident merely started as a result of the presence of the motor vehicle on the road and took on its more criminal elements thereafter." Judge Picton, giving judgment, referred to *R. v Waring* [2005] EWCA Crim 1080; [2006] 1 Cr. App. R. (S.) 9 and *R. v Griffin* [2019] EWCA Crim 563; [2019] 2 Cr. App. R. (S.) 32 (both cited in the main work at para.20-72 as well as *R. v Sofekun* [2008] EWCA Crim 2035; [2009] 1 Cr. App. R. (S.) 78 (see para.20-71 of the main work) and conceded that a court could disqualify under what is now s.163 as an additional punishment. Nevertheless, the appeal was allowed because the court at first instance had given the impression it was sentencing the offender for offences he had been acquitted of (dangerous driving) or offences the Crown had chosen not to pursue (failing to stop and failing to report an accident). The accused had made no comment at interview and had given no explanation for leaving the scene and lying about who had been driving. It is unclear from the judgment of the Court of Appeal whether it would have reached a different conclusion had the DNA tests come back after the six-month time limit for the summary proceedings; in light of *R. v Bains* (above) perhaps it might have done, although it seems unlikely as the court concluded "[w]hilst there is scope for suspicion as to why the appellant chose not to remain at the scene, we do not assess the circumstances as amounting to anything more than that"—*R. v Morgan* [2021] EWCA Crim 1293.

A defendant who committed fraud by insuring his car in his brother's name and went on to pervert the course of justice by reporting that the car had been stolen in an attempt to frustrate a police investigation was disqualified for 12 months under s.146 of the Powers of Criminal Courts (Sentencing) Act 2000. He appealed against that disqualification. The car had been driven dangerously on the motorway; the driver had evaded police in a chase, overtaken other vehicles at 130 mph and travelled at over 100 mph on a 50 mph-limit road. On the next day the appellant falsely reported the theft of the vehicle. The police arrested and interviewed the defendant's brother before discovering the appellant's deception. The appellant denied driving and refused to name the driver, though he admitted to a probation officer that he had been a passenger in the car when it was driven dangerously. The Court of Appeal noted the disqualification should have been imposed under s.163 of the Sentencing Act 2020 (s.146 was repealed when the Sentencing Code came into force) but refused the appeal. The offender was only 17 at the time of the offence, had no previous convictions, had pleaded guilty and was pursuing qualifications in vehicle maintenance meaning that his career might be impeded by the disqualification. Nevertheless, had he been convicted of driving the car he would have received a much heavier sentence (he was given nine months' detention in a young offenders institution suspended for two years with curfew, unpaid work and attendance centre requirements). The appeal court noted that both of his offences were linked to his ownership of the car which had been used by someone with his permission to commit an extremely dangerous offence, the investigation of which the applicant had impeded by his actions. It was not arbitrary in those circumstances to disqualify the applicant from driving. Nor was it arguable that the total sentence was manifestly excessive—*R. v Khan* [2022] EWCA Crim 281.

Disqualification pending passing a driving test

20-77   A passenger guilty of allowing himself to be carried in a vehicle which was driven dangerously resulting in death and who had shown a reckless disregard for any rules relating to the driving of cars met the criterion for disqualification until he had taken an extended driving test as such disqualification was necessary for the protection of the public (see *R. v Beech* [2016] EWCA Crim 1746; [2016] 4 W.L.R. 182)—*R. v Wilson* [2022] EWCA Crim 807; [2022] Crim. L.R. 853.

CHAPTER 22

APPEALS

HIGH COURT

Cases stated

Whether a defendant has a statutory defence of "lawful excuse" when rights **22-32** under the European Convention on Human Rights are engaged in a criminal matter constitutes a question of law about which a magistrates' court may state a case for the opinion of the High Court—*DPP v Ziegler* [2021] UKSC 23; [2022] A.C. 408.

Where a judge in the Crown Court exercises the powers of a District Judge (Magistrates' Courts) under s.66 of the Courts Act 2003, an appeal by way of case stated is an appeal from the Magistrates' Court and not the Crown Court so there is no power to extend the 21-day time-limit for making an application. Nevertheless, where the aggrieved seeks judicial review of the decision, the High Court may grant relief—*R. (on the application of Ogunsola) v Crown Court at Aylesbury* [2021] EWHC 1062 (Admin); [2021] A.C.D. 81. The appellant was charged with an indictable offence and appeared in the Crown Court where the judge sat as District Judge to amend the charge to one which was triable summarily only and one the appellant had previously offered to admit. The appellant pleaded guilty. He then asked the judge to state a case for the opinion of the High Court. The judge refused to state a case and the High Court upheld that refusal (albeit on different grounds—the judge in the Crown Court assumed there was power to extend the time-limit but refused to do so). The High Court, nevertheless quashed the conviction as the judge had no jurisdiction to amend the charge out of time.

Rule 35.3 of the Criminal Procedure Rules 2020 (as amended) now provides for **22-33** the timetable set following a decision by a court to state a case as "15 business days" rather than "21 days".

COURT OF APPEAL

The test as to whether a person may appeal against conviction following a guilty **22-56** plea to an indictment is whether that conviction is unsafe. There are broadly three categories of such cases (although this is not a closed list). The first category includes a variety of circumstances including an equivocal or an unintended plea, a plea of guilty entered as result of an erroneous adverse ruling by the trial judge that left no arguable defence to be put before the jury, and a guilty plea vitiated by improper pressure (e.g. from the judge) or resulting from erroneous legal advice. The second category applies when there is a legal obstacle to the appellant being tried for the offence, such as an abuse of process or where there was a fundamental breach of an accused's rights under art.6 of the European Convention on Human Rights. The third category applies where it is established the appellant did not commit the offence. The test for this third category is not whether there is "legitimate doubt" about the conviction, still less a "lurking doubt"; appellants in such cases must demonstrate that they are not culpable for what they have previously admitted. An important common element across the three categories is that the circumstances relied on must be established by the appellant—*R. v T* [2022] EWCA Crim 108.

INDEX

LEGAL TAXONOMY

FROM SWEET & MAXWELL

This index has been prepared using Sweet & Maxwell's Legal Taxonomy. Main index entries conform to keywords provided by the Legal Taxonomy except where references to specific documents or non-standard terms (denoted by quotation marks) have been included. These keywords provide a means of identifying similar concepts in other Sweet & Maxwell publications and on-line services to which keywords from the Legal Taxonomy have been applied. Readers may find some minor differences between terms used in the text and those which appear in the index. Suggestions to *sweetandmaxwell.taxonomy@tr.com*.

Also available:

Thomas' Sentencing Referencer 2023, *Lyndon Harris*
ISBN: 9780414109193   Publication date: November 2022
Formats: Paperback/ProView eBook/Westlaw UK
Provides clear and concise guidance on the operation of the Sentencing Code with concise summaries of the important case law. With user-friendly tables and flow charts, including tables on guilty plea reductions by percentage and key details of minimum sentences. For many, it is quite simply the usual starting point from which they can confidently find a path through the maze of legislation

Sentencing Principles, Procedure and Practice 2023
Lyndon Harris and Sebastian Walker
ISBN: 9780414108851   Publication date: November 2022
Formats: Hardback/ProView eBook
The essential sentencing text, updated with all the latest changes from the Police, Crime, Sentencing and Courts Act 2022 and all important cases from the Court of Appeal (Criminal Division). The book is split into two parts. Part A contains everything you need to know about sentencing procedure, courts' sentencing powers and sentencing principles. The title has been structured around the Sentencing Code with extensive commentary on the Sentencing Code (as amended) and guidance regarding the extent to which case law pre-dating the Sentencing Code continues to apply. Part B provides guidance on determining the appropriate sentence for almost all criminal offences, including the sentencing guidelines and important cases from the Court of Appeal (Criminal Division). Part B also includes commentary on the approach to determining the appropriate sentence designed to be useful to practitioners and the judiciary.

Class Actions in England & Wales, 2nd edition, *Damian Grave, Maura McIntosh, Gregg Rowan + a team of experts*
Hardback   ISBN: 9780414102552   September 2022
This title is also available on Westlaw UK and as an eBook on Thomson Reuters ProView™

Features of the book include:
- Coverage of various class action procedures and funding, conduct, trial and settlement
- The text draws on applicable procedural rules, case law, comparative analysis and the authors' own experience of class action litigation
- It gives an overview of class actions, including the definition of a class action, the procedures for the grouping of claims and the distinction between opt-in and opt-out claims

- It outlines the principles relating to jurisdiction, choice of law and enforcement of judgments in England and Wales, how they have changed in the light of Brexit, and how they apply in group action context
- The text looks at the participation of foreign claimants and the enforcement of foreign class action judgments or settlement
- It explains how to commence and conduct a group action, including case management, disclosure and evidence, giving examples of cases
- It outlines the trial, judgment and settlement processes of a group action, looking at practical issues
- Costs and third party funding of group actions are explained
- The second edition of this seminal work:
- Adds four new chapters on specific areas of law: insurance, product liability, data class actions and employment;
- Updates the text throughout to reflect case law and developments since publication of the first edition;
- Contains further detail on the representative action procedure under CPR 19.6, and the circumstances in which it may be used in the light of the Supreme Court's decision in Lloyd v Google;
- Completely overhauls the chapter on jurisdiction, choice of law and the recognition and enforcement of judgments to take account of the significant impact of Brexit;
- Adds a particularly large volume of new content to the chapter on competition claims, relating to the Supreme Court's judgment in Merricks v MasterCard and the subsequent decisions in a number of cases that had been on hold while the Supreme Court's judgment was awaited;
- Revises substantially the chapter on environmental and human rights-based claims to reflect the Supreme Court's decisions in Vedanta and Okpabi, as well as the impact of Brexit;
- Updates the chapter on shareholder actions to reflect the decision in the Lloyds/HBOS litigation, which was the first in a shareholder class action in this jurisdiction, and the decision in the Autonomy litigation, which is significant in particular in relation to claims under s.90A of the Financial Services and Markets Act 2000.

Contact us on: Tel: +44 (0)345 600 9355
Order online: sweetandmaxwell.co.uk

Archbold Magistrates' Courts Criminal Practice 2023

19th Edition

General Editor: Stephen Leake

The comprehensive, authoritative and practically focused work for practitioners working in magistrates' courts, youth courts and those working within the wider criminal justice sector. The work provides detailed coverage of the criminal jurisdiction of magistrates' courts and youth courts, together with the growing number of civil orders which complement the criminal jurisdiction. Content is easily accessible, allowing the user to quickly identify key issues and find fast answers to difficult questions. An essential work for all involved in making the system effective: practitioners prosecuting or defending, magistrates, and those responsible for advising them in the administration of the courts. Usable as a stand-alone reference in magistrates' and youth court proceedings.

Hardback
9780414104525
October 2023
£199
This title is also available on Westlaw UK and as an ebook on Thomson Reuters Proview

The new edition includes:

- Nationality and Borders Act 2022
- Policing, Crime, Sentencing and Courts Act 2022
- Judicial Review and Courts Act 2022
- Latest amendments to the Criminal Procedure Rules and Criminal Practice Directions
- New Attorney General's guidelines on disclosure
- Incorporation of increased sentencing powers available to magistrates' courts in respect of either way offence
- References to all new sentencing guidelines
- Consideration of new key cases
- Revised chapter dealing with revenue, customs and immigration offences

ORDER TODAY...   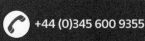 sweetandmaxwell.co.uk   +44 (0)345 600 9355

SWEET & MAXWELL

 **THOMSON REUTERS®**

Archbold Magistrates' Courts Criminal Practice 2023